I0482892

Finding Stocks:

Concise Edition

Tony Pow

Why you want to read this book

It should improve your financial health substantially.

- This book has about 55 pages (6*9) and is about double the size of its competitors with similar price range.

- A best seller was written by a young writer whose main income was from his books and none from his investing. Most of my income is from investing.

- Many popular books claiming the authors making millions. However, usually their techniques are hard to follow. Many admitted they had been bankrupted many times. My techniques minimize risking our money. Paper test your technique first.

- There are many popular books combining technical and some fundamentals. They worked very well at one time and folks making millions following the advices. However, look at their recent performances of the last five years.

- One book describes ROE as the only theme (with the story of the life of the author to fill up the book).

My motivation to write this book

I would like to share my experiences, both good and bad. I use simple-to-follow techniques using the free (or low-cost) resources available to us.

Click the link for the articles I wrote for SeekingAlpha.com, a site for investors. http://seekingalpha.com/author/tony-pow/articles

Contents

Performance of my screens

I monitor the performance of my top screens every 6 months or so. Here is my September, 2013 summary. The purpose is identifying the screens that have performed well recently. It is for illustration purpose only. All returns are annualized. They are sorted by Grand Avg. in descending order.

Screen	Last Monitor 2/13	Current Test Avg.	Long-term Avg.	Short-term Avg.	Grand Avg.	Avail.
EP	39%	66%			59%	75%
BB3	35%	70%			53%	25%
LPSER	-21%	72%			49%	75%
MN	19%	53%			45%	75%
CW	64%	49%	39%	20%	38%	100%
LR	30%	37%			35%	100%
TT	30%	26%	71%	8%	35%	100%
TV2	50%	76%	14%	19%	35%	100%
BFSCB	5%	38%			31%	100%
DO	29%	24%	30%		28%	100%
AR	56%	53%	23%	6%	28%	100%
BE	81%	44%	10%	13%	25%	100%
FA	16%	27%			25%	100%
BS5BV	21%	25%			24%	100%
SE		53%	20%	-3%	23%	100%
CAO	-3%	17%	37%	12%	21%	100%
...	...	...	---	...	...	
Avg.	34%	19%	23%	5%	19%	

Screen.
They are the abbreviations. To illustrate, CAO is the screen looking for candidates for acquisition with low market caps. I have about 25 production screens. They have been selected among over 100 screens.

Last Monitor 2/2013.
Copied from the "Current Test Avg." from my last monitor in 2/2013.

Current Test Avg.

It is the average of the four tests on recent months. The four test dates are: 03/11/13 to 7/9/13, 4/9/13 to 8/7/13, 5/9/13 to 8/17/13 and 6/8/13 to 9/6/13. They are about 4 months apart. It is the most important average to reflect what worked recently.

Long-term Avg.
It is the long-term performance (about 12 months) of the actual, screened stocks. These are stocks that have been actually screened and some may have been purchased.

Short-term Avg.
It is the short-term performance (about 6 months) of the actual, screened stocks.

Grand Avg.
It is a weighted average of the above 4 return categories (Last Monitor, Current Test Avg., Long-Term Avg. and Short-Term Avg.) and they're sorted in descending order.

Run the top screens first as they have given me better returns in the past. It does not guarantee that they will perform as well as before, but they have a better chance to perform well than the screens scored below the average.

Availability.
To illustrate, if the screen found stocks in 1 out of the 4 tests, it is 25% available. These screens may not have enough data for prediction on the future results and there is a higher chance that I will not find any stocks using these screens.

Observations
The following are the personal findings on my own screens. You can do something similar to separate your top screens from the rest of your screens. Test and monitor the performances of your own screens.

- Usually the top half of the screens from the last monitor show up in this monitor though their ranks may vary.

- CAO in the last monitor should be better than it indicates. At least two companies had been acquired and they had very good returns. These two companies did not show up in the test as they're taken out from the historical database; it is termed as survivorship bias.

- CW is quite consistent to the last monitor.

- EP and BB3 have not found any stocks in actual usage. MN proves to be a good screen in these two performance monitors. I missed the opportunities to make good money from this screen – my mistake.

- LPSER is a risky screen demonstrated here and from the previous monitors. I prefer not to take unnecessary risk. Include a column of maximum drawdown as it is a good indicator to avoid risky screens.

- LR was below the average and that's why it had not been used. It is above the average in this monitor, so it will be used to some small extent.

- TT is above the average in these two monitors. The returns of screened stocks during this monitor are better in both long term and short term and hence it will be used.

- The original table (not shown here) has comparisons to SPY (an ETF simulating the market). Beating the market is my yardstick. If most of your screens beat the market, most likely they will beat the market again. However, there are exceptions such as when the market is plunging. In this case, value stocks are better than growth stocks, and cash is the king.

  The market during my last monitor is better than this period. If the return of SPY is negative in the last three months, there is a good chance that the market is trending down.

- There are some screens that just do not perform for a long while. They will not even be monitored next time. However, when the phase of the market cycle changes, the performance of these screens may respond differently.

- The test results are not always consistent. It could be due to my limited data, or the market does not behave normally.

Introduction

There are about 4,000 of stocks (about 30,000 if you include smaller stocks and stocks on foreign exchanges). How can you find the winners? Screening stocks can give you a manageable list of candidates worth your further evaluation.

You can use one of the simple screens that are available to you free from many web sites such as Finviz.com and the one from your broker to find a handful of stocks. The filter criteria could be "P/E < 10", "Sales Growth by 20%" or a combination. If the screens consistently find you winners, they are good.

It is more complicated than that. Otherwise there will be no poor folks. However, most screened stocks should be evaluated. Among the 50 or so screens, there is only one evergreen screen that gives consistent stocks that perform. Some screens work better than others in different phases of the market cycle and/or different market conditions such as during the end of year. You need to use different screens for different purposes. For example, stress on value parameters such as "P/E" for value stocks that have to be held for a longer time than momentum stocks.

Strategies are similar to screening except finding stocks without screening such as finding stocks via headline news. The strategy "Buy and Hold" is dead since 2000.

This book is not written by a journalist (unless you enjoy good English only) but by one who uses screens successfully every week. This book was last updated in 2014, not 20 years ago when the conventional wisdom may have been outdated.

From my real experience, there are screens for different purposes such as stocks for long-term, short-term and momentum. Some screens work better in different phases of a market cycle. We also have to monitor the performance results of our production screens (Chapter 1) to ensure we use are still winners.

You need to perform further qualitative analysis on the identified stocks before you buy them. When we learn, practice and verify all these topics described in this book, the chance of success is far, far better than buying stocks without these disciplines. Avoid tips and recommendations from the media. Most likely they are not useful by the time they reach you.

The strategies described here have been used in my book Best Stocks 2014, According to Me. From 12/16/13 (the publish date) to 3/4/14, the list of all 135 selected stocks beat SPY by 103% and the list of 9 small cap stocks beat SPY by 500%. Past performance is no guarantee to future performance.

The size of this book is measured in pages of 6*9. It does not narrate the story of my life as many other authors do. The exception is when it is related to the topic such as my blunders in investing. It has copied many ideas and provides links to articles from related books and updated articles in the internet.

This book is part of the Concise Series. They include one or few most important chapters from my full-size books. It competes with books with similar size and price.

How this book is organized

Most graphs are in landscape orientation for both paperback and e-readers. Some graphs may not be displayed adequately on a small screen of an e-reader. E-readers may be available in the current version of Windows, so you can read e-books on the larger screen of your PC. For better orientation, just flip the e-readers 90 degrees.

A link is usually included for these screens. Copy it to your browser to display the graphs on your PC if desirable. Instructions on how to produce some graphs are provided as you should try them out. One example is how to produce a chart on detecting market crashes.

It is easier to display some tables in landscape mode, which can be selected in your e-reader.

The font size and page size of most e-book formats can be adjusted. The unknown, special character is the "smiling face" that the current Kindle does not convert correctly.

There are clickable links to web articles. Most of them are from my own web sites and public web sites such as Wikipedia. Some public links may not be available in the future as they are not under my control.

Fidelity Video provides video clips to explain some basic terms and it may require Fidelity customers to sign on in order to view them. Check the trial offer from Fidelity. YouTube offers similar video lessons.

These links extend the usefulness of this book by making available specific topics that may not be interesting to every reader.

The current version provides most of the links the paperback readers can enter into your browser. Get the same information by entering a search in Wikipedia such as Dogs of Dow.

Investopedia is another source beside Wikipedia.
http://www.investopedia.com/

'Afterthoughts' includes my additional comments and comments from others. Readers can make comments in this book's website. These comments may be included in the Afterthoughts in subsequent revisions, with the commenter's last name redacted. It is the section of the article for freer and informal discussion.

For convenience, this book uses SPY, an Exchange Traded Fund (ETF) simulating the S&P 500, as the benchmark for the market.

Annualized returns (Return * 365 / (Days between)) are used where appropriate for more meaningful comparison. To illustrate, I have a 10% return in 6 months, a 10% in a year and a 10% in 2 years. It is more meaningful to use annualized returns of 20%, 10% and 5% respectively for the 6-month return, the one-year return and the 2-year return in this example.

Usually I do not include the dividend, so you can add an estimated 1.5% to the annualized return. In addition, compound interest is not used for easier calculation, so the actual return could be even better.

About the author

I graduated from Cal. State University at San Jose in Industrial Engineering and University of Mass. in Amherst with a MS in Industrial Engineering. My last job was in IT. I have been an investor for over 30 years.

Dedication

To all retail investors and future retail investors. I sincerely hope this book will build bridges with fellow investors with different backgrounds.

Acknowledgement

Thanks to: Seeking Alpha, Fidelity, Wikipedia and Investopedia for the many helpful links to enrich this book.
Yahoo!Finance and Finviz.com for the tools and charts used in this book.

Important notices

© 2014-2021 Tony Pow. Emails to pow_tony@yahoo.com.

Version	E-Book	Paper
1.0	05/14	05/14
2.0	06/19	06/19
2.4	09/21	09/21

Printed version.

ISBN-13 978-1499190502 ISBN-10: 1499190506

No part of this book can be reproduced in any form without the written approval of the author. Book store managers can order this book from Createspace.com.

Book update.

https://ebmyth.blogspot.com/2020/12/updates-for-all-books.html

Disclaimer

Do not gamble money that you cannot afford to lose. Past performance is a guideline and does not guarantee future performance.

All information is believed to be accurate, but nothing is guaranteed. All the strategies described have no guarantee that they will make money and they may lose money. Do not trade without doing due diligence and be warned that most data would be obsolete. All my articles and the associated data are for informational purposes only. I'm not a professional investment counselor or a tax professional. Seek one before you make any investment decision.

The above mentioned also applies for all other advice such as on accounting, taxes, health and any topic mentioned in this book. I am not a professional in any of these fields. Same for all the links contained in this book. Some articles may offend some one or some organization unintentionally. If I did, I'm sorry about that. I am politically and religiously neutral. I try my best effort to ensure the accuracy of my articles. Data also from different sources was believed to be accurate. However, there is no guarantee that they are accurate and suitable for the current market conditions and /or your individual situations. I and my publisher are not liable for any damages in using this book.

Finding stocks

The worst way to find stocks is via TV. Many analysts have hidden agenda. More than one time, a fund manager or an analyst recommended a stock while his company was unloading it. Many have conflicting interests. Some may buy the stock before they recommend it. Unless you have reliable insider information (be warned that it is illegal to use insider information), trust your own research.

1 Where the web sites are

- **Free and simple screen sites**

  They are described in this article or type the following
  http://stocks.about.com/od/researchtools/a/071909screenlist.htm

  - Yahoo!Finance.
    Click here or type
    http://screener.finance.yahoo.com/stocks.html

  - Finviz.
    Click here or type
    http://Finviz.com/screener.ashx

    How to scan using Finviz (YouTube).
    https://www.YouTube.com/watch?v=aQ_0FTg9Cfw

    Screening using technical indicators (particularly useful for momentum stocks).
    https://www.YouTube.com/watch?v=RZRP2NeSX0s

  - Your broker.
    Fidelity's screens are more sophisticated than most.

  - More options: Google, CNBC.com and Moringstar.com.

  Here is a list.
  http://stocks.about.com/od/researchtools/a/071909screenlist.htm

- **Sophisticated screens (usually not free)**

Most of them are more complicated and need time to learn. Both Vector Vest and Stock123 provide historical databases for back testing your screens. Zacks has an earnings revision database at extra cost. GuruFocus has an easy-to-use but powerful screen function.

AAII provides screened stocks from various screens in its low-priced subscription. Both AAII and Value Line take care of some specific industries, but they provide no historical database at least for regular subscriptions. AAII provides historical performance summaries of their screens included in its subscription.

Afterthoughts

Here are the links to screens provided by Marketwatch and NASDAQ.
http://www.marketwatch.com/tools/stockre...
http://www.nasdaq.com/reference/stock-sc...

How to find quality stocks.
http://seekingalpha.com/article/2381395-how-to-identify-quality-stocks-and-is-there-really-alpha-to-be-had

Filler
"Sell in May" could be a self-fulfilled prophecy. I prefer to sell on April 1 and come back on Oct. 15 to avoid the herd.

2   A simple tutorial

From your browser, bring up Yahoo!Finance's screener by clicking here or type http://screener.finance.yahoo.com/stocks.html.

Select the following to select stocks with share price > $5, market cap > 250 mil, P/E < 15, Est. Earning Growths up to 20% for 1 year and up to 5% for 5 years, and Buy Rating = 1.

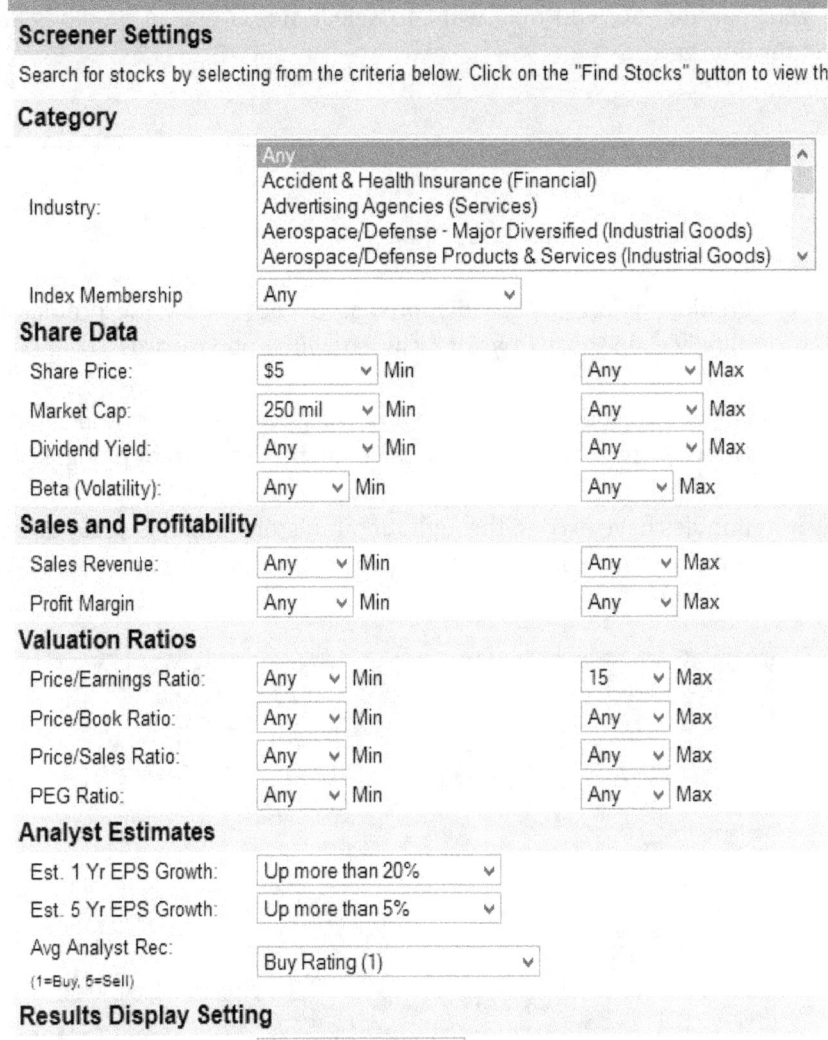

Screener Settings

Search for stocks by selecting from the criteria below. Click on the "Find Stocks" button to view th

Category

Industry:	Any
	Accident & Health Insurance (Financial)
	Advertising Agencies (Services)
	Aerospace/Defense - Major Diversified (Industrial Goods)
	Aerospace/Defense Products & Services (Industrial Goods)

| Index Membership | Any |

Share Data

Share Price:	$5	Min	Any	Max
Market Cap:	250 mil	Min	Any	Max
Dividend Yield:	Any	Min	Any	Max
Beta (Volatility):	Any	Min	Any	Max

Sales and Profitability

| Sales Revenue: | Any | Min | Any | Max |
| Profit Margin | Any | Min | Any | Max |

Valuation Ratios

Price/Earnings Ratio:	Any	Min	15	Max
Price/Book Ratio:	Any	Min	Any	Max
Price/Sales Ratio:	Any	Min	Any	Max
PEG Ratio:	Any	Min	Any	Max

Analyst Estimates

Est. 1 Yr EPS Growth:	Up more than 20%
Est. 5 Yr EPS Growth:	Up more than 5%
Avg Analyst Rec: (1=Buy, 5=Sell)	Buy Rating (1)

Results Display Setting

Click on Find Stocks.

As of 9/21/2013, you cannot find any stocks based on these criteria. Relax the filter by taking out the Est. 1-Yr Growth and the 5-Yr Growth. Click on Find Stocks again. You should find several stocks.

The stocks with '.xx' at the end could be the stocks you may not want to consider. They could be foreign stocks in foreign exchanges, listed in pink sheets, etc. That's why most screens allow you to select Exchanges.

One common problem with this screen is that it may not handle negative or zero earning. So, you may want to select stocks whose earnings are greater than zero.

Tips

- Predictions are just predictions, so do not follow the predictors blindly even those (myself included) with good records.

- No one including all the Federal Reserve chairmen and all the Nobel-Prize winners in economics can predict market plunges.

- Bubbles have existed throughout our history. Bubbles occur due to the excessive valuation initially driven up by the big institutional investors.

3   Finviz's parameters

Most metrics are described in Finviz (via Help), Investopedia and/or Wikipedia and my chapter on P/E. The following are my personal comments and why I feel some metrics are more important than others. Compare the ratios to the companies in the same sector and also its averages from the last 5 years.

From your browser, enter Finviz.com. Enter a symbol (I used ABEO for discussion). A chart is displayed with the prices and volumes for the last nine months. SMAs (Single Moving Average) are displayed sometimes with other technical indicators. Intraday, Daily and Weekly options are available.

Besides the metrics described next and the chart, it describes what the company does, analysts' recommendations (I prefer Fidelity's Equity Summary), insiders' trading and articles that are good for qualitative analysis. "Financial Highlights and Statements" are materials for more in-depth analysis and they were more important decades ago when most financial ratios had not been calculated for you.

The following metrics are roughly based on the flow of Finviz from top to bottom and left to right. I skip those metrics that I believe are not too important. You can also place your cursor on the metric to have the description from Finviz. Some metrics are left blank to indicate they are not applicable (zero, negative or not available). For example, the Debt/Equity of YRCW in 1/2019 is blank (same as null) due to Equity being negative. From Yahoo!Finance, it has a total debt of 888M.

- **Index**. Most of us trade stocks in the three major exchanges in the USA. Stocks listed in over-the-counter are too risky for most of us. Skip the stocks in local exchanges and foreign exchanges if you are not an expert on these stocks. I screen the stocks and then ignore the stocks that are not in the Dow, NASDAC and Amex. Other screeners may let you to select a group of exchanges.

- **Market Cap** (MC). To me, stocks below 50M are risky even if they could be very profitable. Ensure the Avg. Volume is at least 10,000 shares and / or your order is less than 1% of the average volume. Some small stocks are controlled by the owners and have small volumes. In this case you cannot sell your stock easily.

Float = Outstanding shares – Insider shares.

Usually it does not matter as they are typically the same. However, it does for small companies with large insider shares. Most of these owners do not want to sell their family businesses and hence they reduce the chance of being acquired entirely or partially for good prices.

- If **Forward P/E** (a.k.a. Expected P/E) is not provided, use the P/E which is based on the trailing last 12 months (TTM). Alternatively, calculate the E by using the E from P/E and multiplying it by its growth rate. It may not be seasonally adjusted. I prefer Expected P/E (or called Forward P/E) as it provides a better predictability power from my limited research.

  Finviz.com leaves the P/E blank (same as null) if the earnings are negative. In this case, I would check out Yahoo!Finance's EV / EBITDA, which also considers taxes and interests. It is similar to the blank on some metrics, if the Asset is negative even if they seldom occur.

  Earnings Yield is equal to E/P and True Earnings Yield (my term) is EBITDA / EV. It is easier to understand. Compare it to the annual dividend yield of a 10-year Treasury which is quite safe. It is also useful in screening and sorting the screened stocks. If you use P/E instead of E/P, in most cases you need to screen or sort stocks with a clause "P/E > 0". When the P/E is less than 5, be careful and there may be a reason why it is so low. Many bankrupting companies have low P/Es at one time.

  Compare the P/E or Forward P/E with the average P/E for the sector and its average P/E for the last 5 years that are available from Fidelity.com. Some sectors have high P/Es. If the sector is cyclical, the earnings could be affected.

- **Cash / share**. It is used to calculate Pow P/E and Pow EY when EV/EBITDA is not available. To illustrate, if the stock is $10 and it has $10 cash / share without debt (i.e. Debt/Equity = 0), most likely it is underpriced as you can get the whole company for nothing. You should find out why the price is so low. It could be the market ignoring the stock, or there is a serious event happening such as a major lawsuit.

- **Dividend %** is useful for income investors. The payout ratio should not be more than 30% except for matured companies.

- **Recs**. Select stocks with 1 or 2. Do not base your stock selection on this recommendation alone. There have been many bad recommendations that could cost you a fortune in losses. Use Fidelity's Equity Summary Score instead.

- **PEG** is a measure of the growth of P/E and hence a growth metric. It is similar to P/E, but it takes the expected earnings growth rate into account. The lower value is better as long as earnings are positive. If earnings are negative, then the reverse is true. It is a defect in using P/E and PEG and that's why I recommend EY (Earnings Yield) and EYG, earnings yield growth.

  If there are two companies with the same P/E, the one with a better PEG ratio is better. If two companies have the same E/P, the company with higher Earnings Growth (EPS Q/Q) would be better.

- **P/B**. Book value (= Total Assets – Total Liabilities) may not include intangible assets such as patents. Do not trust it 100%, so is ROE which is based on book value. Negative equity is possible when Total Liabilities is more than Total Assets. This popular metric is outdated for most matured companies as it is now made up of intangible assets including patents, management, the quality of employees, brand names, market share, partners, free cash flow and customer base.

- **P/S**. If two companies are unprofitable, this ratio can be used. I prefer profitable companies.

- **P/FCF**. I prefer it to be greater than 0 and less than 50 for value investors. Most metrics can be manipulated easily, but not this one.

- **Sales Q/Q** reduces the seasonal deviation. To illustrate, retail sales for the Christmas season should be compared to the same season in the prior year.

- **EPS Q/Q**. Same as above. I prefer the growth of EPS over Sales. Both of these Q/Q ratios are growth metrics. When a company terminates its unprofitable product(s), its Sales Q/Q could be down but its EPS Q/Q could be up. In 2000, many internet companies had great Sales Q/Qs but negative EPS Q/Qs.

Q/Q comparison (quarter to quarter) takes out the seasonal variations.

When the company buys its own shares, EPS could be misleading as E is fixed and the number of shares is reduced. In most cases, the fundamentals of the company have not changed.

- Positive **Insider** Transactions are favorable. Sometimes, they are misleading. Need to scroll to the end of the screen and check out more info there. If the transactions are outdated such as 3 months or so ago, and or they are purchases in a similar amount than the sales a while ago, they are not important. Insiders know the company better than us. So is Institutional Transactions as institutional investors move the market.
- Insider Own, Shares Outstanding and Shares **Float** determine the number of shares that are available for trading. A small Float with a high Insider Own limits trading and the stock should be avoided in most cases. Compare your trade position for the stock to the Avg. Volume.
- **Profit Margin**. I prefer it over Gross Margin and Oper. Margin which does not include interest expenses and taxes. When you sell software, the Gross Margin is high as it does not include development, support and marketing, etc. A retail store has low Gross Margin. It all depends on the industry, and hence it is better to compare companies in the same industry.
- **Short Float**. I prefer it to be less than 10%. If it is greater than 10%, the shorters could find something wrong with the company. If it is over 25%, I would check the fundamentals. If they are good, I would buy expecting a short squeeze potential. It has been risky but proven to be profitable for me.
- Technical metrics: SMA-20, SMA-50 and SMA-200. Finviz expresses them in convenient percentages. If they are all positive, it means the trend is up. SMA-20 is a short-term trend and SMA-200 is a long-term trend. If you are a short-term swing investor, stick with the short-term trend and vice versa. The first two are momentum grades. Many long-term investors do not buy stocks when the SMA-200% is negative.
- **RSI(14)**. If it is greater than 65%, it is overbought. If it is under 30%, it is under-bought for me. Some use 5% up or down than mine. Use it as a reference. Most stocks making new heights are always overbought, and many of these stocks keep on rising. I recommend using trailing stops to protect your profit.

- **Beta**. A volatile stock fluctuates a lot. It is good for short-term traders. A beta of 1 means the stock would fluctuate with the market, and be volatile if it is higher than 1. For volatile stocks (higher than 1), the stops should be higher. For example, if your stops are normally 5%, you may want to use 7% or even higher.
- Management performance is measured by ROE. It is also judged by **Analysts' Rec.** and Institutional Ownership (except for small companies). The confidence of their own ability, the company and its sector is measured by Insider Ownership and Insider Purchases.

  ROE = Net Income / Average Shareholder's Equity
  According to Investopedia, a normal ROE for utilities should be 10% while high tech companies should be 15%. Compare this ratio and many other ratios with its peers that are available from Fidelity.
- Avoid all companies that are going to bankrupt at all costs. Debt/Equity, P/FCF, Cash/Sh., P/B, Profit Margin, Forward P/E, Short Float, RSI(14), SMA20% and SMA50 would give us hints. Need to summarize all the info and study many other factors such as obsoleting products (including drugs).
- Unless you have concrete information, do not buy stocks a week or so before the Earnings Date.

More useful information:

- The price chart. It has a lot of features such as the resistance line. Some charts include technical indicators such as double top (a bearish warning) and double bottom (a bullish sign).
- Description under the symbol. It briefly describes what the company (sector and industry) does and its country of registration. You want to buy a stock within a sector that is trending up. For example, according to Finviz Apple is in the Consumer Goods sector and the Electronic Equipment industry.

  If you do not want to buy foreign stocks, skip it if it is not listed in the US exchange.
- Articles on the company for qualitative analysis.
- Insider trading. Pay more attention to the insider purchases at market prices. Use common sense.
- The last line lets you open Yahoo!Finance and other sites.

Your broker's website

Your broker website should have plenty of tools to analyze stocks. As of Dec., 2018, Fidelity lets you use their extensive research free by opening an account with no position restriction. I describe some of their metrics that should be beneficial to your research.

- Equity Summary Score. Potentially good buy when it is 7 (8 for conservative investors) or higher. With some exceptions, you should avoid or short stocks if the score is 3 or below. The stocks ranking from 4 to 6 could be turnaround candidates if they are supported by good Q/Q Earnings and/or good news.

- The 5-year averages are good yardsticks. For example, in Dec., 2018, C's P/E is about 9 and the average is 14. Hence it is a value buy.

Other sources

If you have other sources (most require a subscription or being a customer), skip the stocks that have one of the failing grades. The exceptions are a new positive development and increased insider purchases.

Vendor	Grade	Fail
Fidelity	Equity Summary Score	< 7
IBD	Composite grade	< 50
Value Line	Proj. 3-5 yr. return. Also its composite rating	< 3%
Zacks	Rank	5
Vector Vest	VST	< 0.7

You may be able to find Value Line and IBD in your library. Try out the free stock reports from your broker first. Finviz and Seeking Alpha should have articles (now fewer free articles from Seeking Alpha) on stocks and earnings conferences, which could have important information after separating from the "welcome" and garbage talks.

Yahoo!Finance has good info. "EV/EBITDA" is better than "P/E" as it considers debts and cash. Most use Earnings from last 12 months, which has poorer predictability than Forward Earnings to me.

When negative values such as Equity on Finviz.com, we need to adjust many related metrics or do not use them at all.

MarketWatch.com has many articles on the market in general and personal investing.

If the stock is close to the Earnings Date (found on Finviz.com), you should avoid trading the stock; as earnings could have a big swing for the stock price. Consult Zacks' ranking which is currently free for individual stocks.

Gurus

It is nice to know how gurus would rate the interested stocks. GuruFocus is a good source. NASDAQ is a simplified version, but it is currently free. Bring up Nasdaq.com from your browser. Select "Investing" and then "Guru Screeners". On the third selection, enter the stock symbol such as THO. Click "Go". You will find how 10 or so gurus would evaluate this stock in theory. Click "Detailed Analysis" for each guru.

Quick and dirty

Many times we need to evaluate a stock fast such as taking action due to some development. Refer to my other article "Simplest way to evaluate stocks". The following should take a few minutes. Bring up Finviz.com and enter the stock symbol.

Using SWKS on 6/10/16 to illustrate, Forward P/E is about 11 (fine between 3 and 25), Debt/Eq. is 0 (fine less than .5), ROE is 30% (fine greater than 5%) and P/PCF is 31 (fine if not negative).

Also, check out Market Cap, Avg. Volume, Dividend, Short Float (fine between 0% and 10%), Country and Industry. Judging from the above, it is a buy.

If you have more time, check out the following: Recom. (Ok if less than 2.5), P/B (fine between .5 and 4), Sales Q/Q (fine if not negative), EPS Q/Q (fine if not negative), Cash/Sh (compare it to Debt/Sh) and Profit Margin (fine >5%). Check some articles described for this stock.

5-minute stock evaluation

It takes even less time than the above "Quick and Dirty". However, I recommend you should spend more time researching stocks.

- From Finviz.com, enter the stock or ETF symbol. Look at the number of reds in metrics. If there are more than greens, most likely it is not a good stock.

- It should be fine if Fidelity's Equity Summary Score is greater than 8.

If you have more time, I recommend you to check the following:

- Check out Forward P/E (E>0 and P/E < 20), Debut / Equity (< 50%) and P/FCF (not in red color).

  If time is allowed, replace Forward P/E with True P/E (same as "EV/EBITDA"), which is available from Yahoo!Finance and other sources.

- SMA20 (or SMA50 for longer holding period). If SMA20 is > 10%, it is trending up.

- It is fine if the Insider Transaction is positive.

- Be cautious on foreign stocks and low-volume stocks.

- If most of the above are positive, it is likely a buy. As in life, nothing is 100% certain.

Links
PEG: http://en.wikipedia.org/wiki/PEG_ratio
Short %:
http://www.investopedia.com/university/shortselling/shortselling1.asp#axzz2LNDvpemo
Openinsider: http://www.openinsider.com/
Finviz: http://Finviz.com/
terms: http://www.Finviz.com/help/screener.ashx
Insider Cow: http://www.insidercow.com/
Current Ratio: http://en.wikipedia.org/wiki/Current_ratio
How to find quality stocks.
http://seekingalpha.com/article/2381395-how-to-identify-quality-stocks-and-is-there-really-alpha-to-be-had

4   Simplest way to evaluate stocks

Beginners should trade ETFs only. This chapter is for the readers who are ready or getting ready to trade stocks.

Many stock researches have already been done recently and some are available free of charge. I have no affiliation with Fidelity except I retired from it. You can open an account with them with no balance. Their Equity Summary Score is one of the best indicators; I check out **value** stocks with score higher than 8.

Several sources

The popular ones are Morningstar, Value Line, The Street and Zacks (currently free for rankings of individual stocks). If they are not free, check out whether they are available from your local library. I have 3 simple ways to evaluate stocks starting with the simplest. In addition, read the articles on the selected stocks from Fidelity, Finviz, Seeking Alpha and many other sources for further evaluation.

Fidelity

Select only stocks that have Fidelity's Equity Summary Score 8 or higher. There are tons of information about a stock.

A modified stock selection based on a magazine article

Most metrics are available from Finviz.

1. Forward P/E (expected earnings and not based on the last twelve months). It should range from 5 to 15 (10 to 25 for high tech stocks). EV/EBITDA (from Yahoo!Finance) is a better choice as it includes the debts and cash than P/E; it would be more effective if it uses forward earnings. If you do not use EV/EBITDA, ensure Debt/Equity is less than 0.5 except for the debt-intensive industries.

2. ROE (Return of Equity) measures how well the company uses the capital. I prefer stocks with ROE greater than 5%.

3. Volatility. Conservative investors should select stocks with a beta of less than one (i.e. less volatile).

4. Insider Transactions from should be less than 5%.

5. Momentum. Check out the SMA-50 (actually SMA-50%) and SMA-200. Ideally they should be positive. It is especially important for stocks you do not want to keep for a long time.

A simple scoring system using Finviz

Bring up Finviz.com and then enter the stock symbol.

No.	Metric	Good	Bad	Score
1	Forward P/E[1]	Between 2.5 and 12.5, Score = 2	> 50 or < 0, Score = -1	
2	P/ FCF[1]	< 12, Score = 1	>30 or < 0, Score = -1	
3	P/S[1]	< 0.8, Score = 1	< 0, Score = -1	
4	P/ B[1]	< 1, Score = 1	< 0, Score = -1	
	Compare quarter to quarter of last year			
5	Sales Q/Q	> 15%, Score = 1	< 0, Score = -1	
6	EPS Q/Q	> 20% , Score = 1	< 0, Score = -1	
			Grand Score	
	Stock Symbol Date[2]	Current Price	SPY	

Footnote

[1] Negative values for Sales (due to accounting adjustments), Equity and Book are possible but not likely.

[2] The last row is for your information only. SPY is used to measure whether it will beat the market by comparing the return of this stock to the return of SPY.

The Score

Score each metric and sum up all the scores giving the Grand Score. If the Grand Score is 3, the stock passes this scoring system. Even if it is a 2, it still deserves further analysis if you have time. You may want to add scores from other vendors. To illustrate on using Fidelity, add 1 to the score if Fidelity's Equity Summary score is 8 or higher. Monitor the performance after every 6 months or so to see whether this scoring system beats the market.

Very basic advice for beginners

Beginners should stick with U.S. stocks with Market Cap greater than 800 M (million), Debt/Equity less than .25 (25%) except for debt-intensive industries such as utilities and airlines and Forward P/E between 5 to 20 (25 for high-tech companies). These metrics are all available from Finviz.com, which is free.

Do not have more than 20% of your portfolio in one stock (unless it is an ETF or mutual fund) and do not have more than 30% of your portfolio in one sector.

For more conservative investors, buy non-volatile stocks whose beta (available from Yahoo!Finance) is less than 1. Beta of 1 represents the market (the S&P 500 index). For example, a stock with beta 1.5 statistically fluctuates more than 50% of the market and hence it is very volatile.

Try paper trading to check out your strategy and your skill in trading stocks. If your broker does not provide one, use a spreadsheet to record your trades or check the availability of simulator.investopedia.com.

Filler 12 noon is not 12 pm

The Chinese restaurant I went to says they are open at 12 am. Are they wrong or is the world wrong?

The next hour after 11 am is 12 am, NOT 12 pm. The one who set it up did it totally wrong and no one complains about it until now. If I were born earlier, I would have corrected it.

5   Fidelity

Fidelity offers a strong screen function. The most unique feature is incorporating its Equity Summary Score (used to be Analyst's Opinion) and some outside researches such as Zacks and Ford.

From the main menu, select "News and Research", "Screen and Filter" and then "Start a screen".

The following example selects stocks with the following criteria: Security Price (2 to 250), Market Cap. (300 and above), Equity Summary Score (8 and above), Zacks (Strongest) and Ford (Strongest).

It displays the 10 stocks. Research each stock. Read the News about each stock. You may want to use Finviz.com, Yahoo!Finance and other sources to double check.

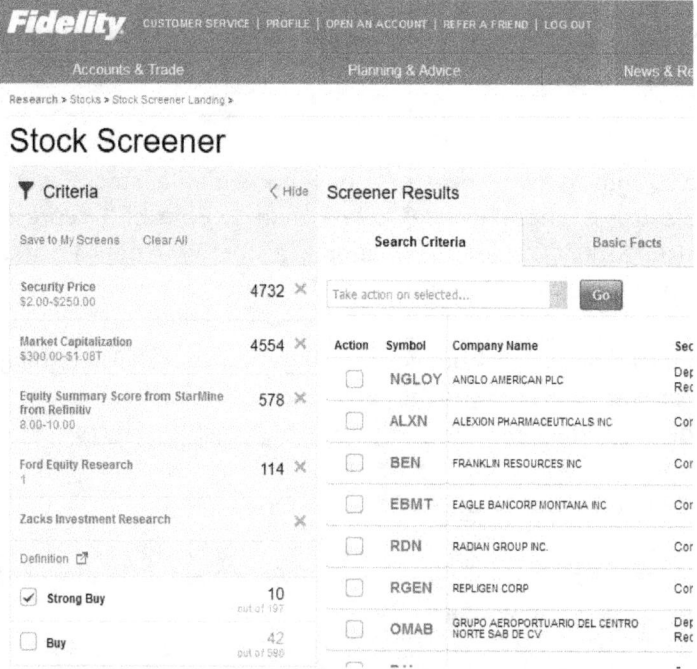

The following describes some of the features.

● Equity Summary Score. It is one of the major metrics I use in my proprietary scoring systems. They are not available to many small stocks. From my limited database in 7/2015 and for short durations, the results are:

Short Term: (7% return for the average)

Metric	Parm. 1	No. of Stocks	%		Parm. 2	No.	%	Predictability
Fidelity Analyst	Buy	150	10%		Sell	279	3%	Good

Long Term: (8% return for the average)

Metric	Parm. 1	No. of Stocks	%		Parm. 2	No.	%	Predictability
Fidelity Analyst	Buy	90	17%		Sell	208	4%	Good

It has its own limits, but they are very minor to me.

First, it does not have a historical database for verifying the screen performance such as the return after a year. However, I do not know any site that provides this function free. To work around this, I save the results in a spread sheet and update the performance.

Secondly, it does not provide many other filter criteria that can be found in other systems such as technical indicators or insider transactions found on Finviz.com. I use other sites for further evaluation.

Most investors should find that this screening is a very good tool and very easy to use.

6   A scoring system

This scoring system helps you to select whether you should buy a stock or not. In this system, when a stock scores higher than 2, it is a buy. As a group, the highly-scored stocks usually perform better than the lowly-scored stocks in a year. The basic concepts are described here.

An Example

For illustration purposes, we use two metrics: Forward P/E and ROI.

First we convert Forward P/E into Forward E/P by flipping the two values. Assuming Forward E/P should have a higher weight than ROI, multiply E/P by 5. The average ROI is 10% (simplified for illustration), so minus it by .1.

Score = Forward E/P * 5 + (ROI -.1)

For example, a stock has a P/E of 10 (E/P = 1/10= .1) and ROI is expressed as 25%.

Score = .1 * 5 + (.25 - .1) = .5 + .15= .65

Some parameters by some sites are expressed in grade such as A, B, C and D. For simplicity, if it is A, then the value is 2 otherwise it is zero.

Score = if (Grade = "A", 2, 0) + ...

Test your system on paper with at least 3 months of data. Check whether your scoring system works. It works when the higher the score corresponds to the better the return. Adjust the weight on each metric and see whether your scoring system improves its predictability.

Again, it is simplified for educational and illustration purpose. Try even more different metrics and check whether the metrics still work in the current market. The next metrics to include could be Equity Summary Score from Fidelity, Debt/Equity and Quarter-to-Quarter Earnings / Sales.

Monitor your scoring system

I am sure that many have tried to use most of the metrics and they still cannot find the Holy Grail. I believe the predictability power of each metric is influenced by the current market conditions. For example, the fundamental metrics such as P/E predict better than the growth metrics such as PEG during the market bottom. You should test the performance of each metric every 6 months or so.

You may have two scores: one for short term and one for long term. The stocks you want to keep in the short term may not be the same kind of stocks you want to keep in the longer term. Short term is 3 months (one month for me) and long term is 12 months for me. My definitions could be different than yours. Value metrics are more important for the long term while growth metrics are more important for the short term.

However, 12 months is too long a period of time and during this period the market may change, so it is better to change it from 12 to 6. To illustrate, energy stocks were great in 2007, but they plunged in 2008. If your scoring system for long-term holding was constructed based on 12 months' data in 2007, the system would have been misleading in 2008 for energy stocks in this example.

I find the short-term scores have a better prediction power than the long-term scores. However, I keep profitable stocks more than 12 months to qualify for the better tax treatments in taxable accounts, and sell the losers less than 12 months. Evaluate the purchased stocks every 6 months to decide whether you want to keep them for another 6 months. Use stops and trialing stops (for winners) to protect your portfolio.

Besides monitoring the metrics in your scoring system, monitor the scores.

The market is not always rational

Sometimes the scoring system fails: When the poorly-scored stocks perform better than the highly-scored stocks. The market is not always rational. Most scoring systems depend on fundamental metrics. When the market switches its favor from value to growth, adjust the score system accordingly. I have found that more than one time that the stocks scored in the top 5% did not perform, so be careful or skip the top 5% (sometimes 10%). The events such as a pending lawsuit or an expiring drug do not show up in metrics, and that is why we need to do other analysis such as Intangible Analysis.

Some metrics almost always work such as the positive predictions of excessive insider's purchases. The insiders know the company typically better than others. When they buy their own company's stock at market prices, they must know it has good appreciation potential. They have many reasons to sell their company's stocks. However, when they sell a large percent of their holdings, be cautious.

When the stock loses more than 30% in a month and you cannot find valid reasons, it may be a good indicator for potential appreciation ahead. Some suggestions are:

- Do not modify your scoring system during market plunges.
- The best strategy is to use the screens (same as searches) that have worked well for the last 90 days.
- Find out why your fundamental metrics that used to work do not work now. You may want to add more weight on growth metrics, and vice versa on value metrics.

An example of monitoring the metrics

This is what I found in monitoring the performances of the metrics as of 3/2013. It is based on a limited database of about 300 stocks with holding periods varying from 1 to 15 months. It has an average of 8% (16% for shorter term). The following is for educational purpose only.

1. The foreign stocks are not doing well: South America (average return is -21% for 7 stocks), Israel (-18% for 2), China (-10% for 7). Europe (0% for 17) and Canada (5% for 16, and most are in natural resources). If I ignore the foreign companies, the return of the portfolio would be increased substantially.

2. The following metrics work fine for the long term only: Forward (same as Expected) Earnings Yield (E/P) and Fidelity's Equity Summary Score.

3. P/B. The stocks with P/B less than 1 perform better than the stocks with P/B greater than 2 (10% vs. 4%).

4. There are no definitive conclusions on Cash / Market Cap, PEG and Return of Equity (a surprise to me) in this monitor.

5. The stocks that were cheaper by 50% to their average 5-year P/E (available from Fidelity) have performed better than those stocks that were cheaper by less than 2%.

6. The ratio of Short / Market Cap between 25% and 30% has better performance than other percentages. It is a contradictory ratio and it could be a short squeeze (a condition that the stock is running out of shares to sell short).

7. There are many composite scores from different vendors that I subscribe to and they are not disclosed here.

8. Based on the above, I will modify my scoring system. I will still have two scores, one for short term and one for longer term.

Short-term scoring system

The scoring system should work better in the shorter term. For testing this system, I used the above data base, but deleted stocks that have been over 8 months old. It is still a small data base of about 190 stocks.

The result is different from the above as the time frame has been reduced. Here is the summary.

1. The predictability of screens (same as searches) performs about the same as the last monitor. A few screens are better than others. I will not use the under-performing screens with real money.

2. The stock grades from several vendors are not a good indicator this time.

3. Expected (same as Forward) Earnings Yield (E/P) has been a good indicator.

4. Cash Flow is a good indicator (different from the last monitor).

5. Fidelity's Equity Summary Score is a good indicator. Finviz has a similar score, but I prefer to use Fidelity's. Fidelity places higher weight on opinions from analysts that have a better prediction on this stock than

others. It eliminates some of the conflict of interest between the analysts and the investing banks s/he works for.

6. The Short Percentage between 25 and 30 is a good contrary indicator (could be a good chance for a short squeeze).

   Its value of less than 10 % is a good indicator. The rest of the range is not conclusive.

7. Cash / Market Cap, Insider Purchase, P/B, ROE and Dividend stocks (>3%) are not conclusive in this monitor.

8. P/S with values less than 0.8 are a good indicator.

9. For some reason I do not know why and how to explain: the top 10% of the top-scored stocks did not perform better than the other stocks that pass.

   It happens in both my two scoring systems. Be suspicious of them and it has happened for more than once. However, the stocks that scored in the bottom 10% are consistently poor performers and that's a good indicator.

There are many other parameters that may be of interest to you. Include them in the performance monitor.

7   Intangibles

I give a score for each stock I evaluate. Occasionally some stocks with poor scores have great returns and vice versa. In general, the scoring system works. It has been proven statistically and repeatedly from my limited data. I stick with high-score stocks with some exceptions.

Once in a while I change my scoring system to adapt to the current market conditions. To illustrate, the market bottom phase and early recovery phase of the market cycle favor value more than momentum/growth. Here are some of my recent experiences and strategies:

- I double or even triple my stake on stocks with high scores. In the longer term, they are consistently better winners than the average with some minor exceptions. Besides the score, look at the intangibles described in this article.

- Watch out for the stocks with outrageous metrics such as P/E of 4 or less. It could be a big lawsuit pending, an expiration of some important drugs, etc. Also, be careful with scores in the top 5%. From my statistics they do worse than the average. Their problems may not show up in the current financial statements.

- The technology of a tech company cannot be ignored even though the company's P/E is high, that I set a limit of 25 instead of 20 for other stocks. The value of the company's technology and patents will not be shown in the fundamental metrics except from the insiders' purchases at market prices.

  For example, IDCC rose about 40% in 2 days. There was a rumor that Google was buying the company and/or Apple was bidding on it too for its mobile technology. Charts usually would flag this kind of event. For non-charters, use the SMA-20% from Finviz.com. They could be a little late as the charts depend on rising prices.

- There are more acquisitions during a market bottom (same as early recovery). The companies with good technologies are bargains and the larger companies especially those in the same sector understand their values better than most of us. These potentially profitable companies will not be shown by their scores explicitly. When corporations have a lot of cash or the credit is cheap, they are looking for smaller companies to acquire or invest in. The candidates are usually small, beaten up, low-priced and having valuable intangible assets such as technologies, customer base and/or market share of the industry segment. 2009-2012 was just the perfect environment and the before that was 2003. I had at least one stock in each of these periods and they appreciated a lot.

- The opposite is Netflix, Chipotle in 1/2012 and Amazon in 1/2013. They are overpriced by any measure. However, the mentioned companies are investing in the future. The shorters (not for beginners) are having a tough time making money on them. When their P/Es are higher than 40, watch out. Some could be OK in the mentioned companies, but usually they are not. Do not follow the herd and your due diligence will verify whether they will still go up.

  Use reward/risk ratio. It is based on experiences. To illustrate, if the company has the equal chance to go up 50% and go down 25%, then it is a buy and the reverse is a sell.

- The retail investor just cannot possibly know about some events until they actually happen. For example, ATSC dropped 15% due to losing its second primary customer. Fundamentals cannot predict this kind of event. Charts can signal this event, but usually they are too late unless you watch the chart all day long.

- After a quick run up, TZOO plunged due to missing some negligible earning expectations. It seems the original climbing prices already had the perfect earnings growth built-in.

  I do not understand why a company loses 10% of its market cap when it missed by 1% of the expected earnings. It could be driven up and down by the institutional investors. Evaluate the stock before you act. Acting opposite to the institutional investors could be very profitable for the right stocks. Avoid trading before the earnings announcement dates (about 4 times a year for most stocks).

- The following are not easily found in financial statements: industry outlook, patents, good will, market share, competition, product margins, management quality, lawsuits pending, potential acquisition, pension obligations, advertising icons, etc. That is why we need to read articles on the stocks in our buy list or our purchased stocks.

- The financial data could be fraudulent or manipulated. I do not trust small companies in emerging markets. I have been burned too many times. Check the company names such as foreign names, ADR and their headquarter addresses (from the company profile in most investing sites).

  Earnings can be manipulated with many accounting tricks. A jump in earnings from last year may not be as rosy as it looks. Check the footnotes in the accounting statements. I usually skip financial statements unless I have big purchases in mind as my time in investing is limited.

- Cash flow cannot be easily manipulated. It is good information whether the company will survive or not, but to me it does not prove to be a consistent predictor in my tests, but an important red flag for companies on their way to bankruptcy. Examples abound.

- Repeated one-time, non-recurring and extraordinary charges are red flags.

- Stay away from the companies where the CEOs are over-compensated. As of 7- 2013, Activision's CEO raised his salary by more than 600%, while the stock lost its value in double digits.

- Value stocks. Need to know why they become value stocks (i.e. fewer investors want to own them) even if they are fundamentally sound. For example, there are two primary reasons for the downfall of a supplier to Apple: 1. Apple is declining in sales and 2. Apple is switching suppliers to replace their product. Technology companies are continually building better mouse traps. They could turn around in a year or so with better products.

Conclusion

Buying a stock is an educated guess that its stock price will rise. Fundamentals do not always work, but they work most of the time:

1. When we buy a value stock, we're swimming against the tide. Hence, we need to wait longer (usually more than 6 months) for the market to realize its value. The exception is the Early Recovery phase (see the

Market Cycle chapter) and it has faster and larger returns than most other stocks from most other stages of the market cycle.

2. Some metrics are misleading. Book value could be misleading for an established company such as IBM. The image of the cowboy in a tobacco company could be a very important asset that is not included in its financial statement.

3. The market is not always rational.

Afterthoughts

*   Brand names of big companies are one of the most important intangibles. Here is a strategy to buy big companies in a down market. It has been proven that it works. However, do not just buy these companies without analysis.
    http://seekingalpha.com/article/1324041-buying-brand-names-in-a-bear-market-can-make-you-rich

*   The reputation of a company takes a long time to build but a bad incident to destroy in the case of GM such as the delay in recalling the killer switches.

#Filler: Carrie Fisher, another sad American story

Unless drug addiction is part of the culture now as evidenced from the legalization of certain drugs, we're in a permissive society! Brits pushed opium as a nation when they had nothing better to trade. Opium killed millions of Chinese and bankrupted China. When we do not learn from history, we will repeat history. It is another sad story of fame and money and then losing it all. I bet she would be happier in a normal life instead of being born in a privileged class. Same can be said for many celebrities such as Presley, Houston and her daughter. RIP.

8   Qualitative analysis

This is the last analysis to evaluate a stock fundamentally. Then the next is technical analysis which is used to find an entry point (also the exit point) for the stock. The market is not always rational. It also depends on the available of money such as easy credit to pump up the market.

Where quantitative analysis fails and why

I find that some stocks with high scores fail and some stocks with low scores succeed as indicated by my performance monitor. The scoring system still works statistically for the majority of my stocks.

- Reasons why stocks with low scores perform:

   o   Oversold. The institutional investors (fund managers and pension managers) dump them first, and then followed by the retail investors. These big boys will buy these stocks back when they reach a certain price range. RSI(14), a technical indicator described in the Technical Analysis article and is available from many sites including Finviz, is useful to detect these oversold stocks.

   o   The falling price (P) improves all fundamental metrics that have the stock price such as P/E and P/Sales. However, the trend of the price is down. Improving Forward P/E is usually a good hint.

   o   The company has turned around after fixing its problems and/or the market has changed for the better. A new management team could improve profitability such as recalling Steve Jobs for Apple.

   o   The current problems have been resolved but not known to the public that could be evidenced by the increase in Insiders' Purchases (from Finviz to start). It includes resolving a lawsuit, a new product, a new drug, or a new big order, etc.

   o   Heavy purchases by insiders. The company's outlook is not shown in its financial statements. Sometimes the insiders hide them so they can buy more of their companies' stocks for themselves.

- Reasons why stocks with high scores plunge in addition to the described in the previous discussion:

  - The company's fundamentals and its prices have reached or closed to the maximum heights. They have no way to go but down. It is particularly true when the stock's timing rating is at or close to the highest point. TTWO that I gifted to my grandchildren had been 5-baggers in the last few years before it plunged in 2018.

  - It has reached its potential value (or a target price) and it is time for many investors to take profits.

  - Sector (or finding another stock or sector with better appreciation potential)) rotation, particularly by institutional investors who drive the market.

    - The outlook of the company, its sector and/or the market is deteriorating. Most companies with P/E less than 5 have problems, and you need to find out the reasons why the stocks are so cheap. Via Finviz, check out debt / share (more than 0.5), negative Q-Q Sales, negative Q-Q Profits, and/or outdated products like typewriters.

  - The stock price may be manipulated. There are many reasons to pump and dump the stock. Shorting is not recommended for most investors. However, some experienced shorters make money consistently when they find valid reasons to short stocks.

  - It could be due to a new serious lawsuit, a new competing product or drug, canceling a major order, etc.

  - Downgrade by analysts. They could spot some bad events such as product defects, violations of regulations or accounting errors / frauds. The downgrades are more important than the upgrades that could have conflict of interest.

  - The financial statement had been manipulated. The SEC may ask for an investigation.

  - Does not meet the consensus in earnings announcements, which have been over-acted by many investors.

Qualitative Analysis

We need to do further analysis after the quantitative analysis and the intangible analysis. Check out the company's prospects. Check out the date of the article and any potential hidden agenda items from the author. Older articles may not have much value.

Be careful on 'pump-and-dump' manipulation written by authors with a hidden agenda. It has happened especially on small companies before even SeekingAlpha.com has its share. Here was an article that tells you to sell NHTC. There was another article to tell you to buy ARTX. They fit into this category.

The sources are:

1. Seeking Alpha.
    Type the symbol of the company to read as many articles on the company as you have time for. Today this site and many other similar sites require you to be a paid member. If you cannot find too many good articles, check out the articles from Finviz.com.

    Recently, I read an article on AMD and it said it may have good profits in the next two years with the game consoles. The outlook of a company is not shown by any fundamental metric which are far from favorable.

    Following a well-known writer, I bought IBM without doing my due diligence (my fault). It went down more than 15% quickly. You can learn from my mistakes.
2. Research reports from your broker. If you do not find many, open an account with one that provides such reports. Some subscription services such as Value Line provide such reports.
3. Yahoo!Finance board. Most comments are garbage. However, once in a while you find some great insights. Usually you cannot find any info from other sources on tiny companies.
4. The most recent company's financial statements. They are usually available from the company's website.
5. 10-Ks from Edgar database (www.sec.gov/edgar). Check out new products and its potential competition, key customers, order backlog, research and development and pending lawsuits.

6. Check out the outlook of the sector the company is in and the company itself.
7. Check out its competitors.
8. Some companies are run by stupid people. I received information via my email saying that my mutual fund account could be treated as an abandoned property. I have been cashing dividend checks every year and why it would be considered as an abandoned property. I called them right away to close my account.

The tall and handsome guy presented articulately how he would turn around JC Penny on TV. I could tell you right away that all his tricks had been tried by other companies such as Sears, and most did not work. The intelligent investor does not care about how handsome, how articulate, how rich his family is and how many advanced degrees from prestigious colleges he possesses. If he does not make sense, do not buy his preaching and his company's stock. [Update. As of 5/2020, J.C. Penny filed for bankruptcy protection. If you had this stock and my book, you would have saved a lot of money minus $10 for my book!]

9. Check out its business model. Some business models do not make business sense and some do. Here are some samples.
- Giving razors makes sense, as the customers have to buy the blades eventually and keep on buying blades for life.
- Supermarket M lowers prices on common merchandise such as Coke and it works. They make money by providing inferior (but profitable to them) products that you cannot compare prices easily such as meat and seafood.

Eventually there will be a supermarket in my area to satisfy me both in price and quality or at least make a good tradeoff.
- Last week it had been brutally hot. I went to a Barnes & Noble's bookstore to enjoy reading the updated books and enjoyed the air conditioning. When there are more free loaders like me than customers, this business model does not work.
- Market dumping works to capture the market. Microsoft used to do it with their new Office and Mail products that could not compete with the established products at the time. Google is following the same model to dump its equivalent products to compete with Office. Now, Microsoft is taking a dose of the same medicine. As of 2015, Google is not winning.

9   Simplest market timing

Market timing depends on charts; the following describes how to use chart information without creating charts. Most charts will not identify the peaks and bottoms of the market as they depend on data (i.e. the stock prices). However, it would reduce further loses. It is simpler than it sounds. Just follow the procedure below.

The first part of this technique detects market plunges, and the second part advises you when to reenter the market. I have modified them.

How to detect market plunges without charts (a.k.a. Death Cross)

1. Bring up Finviz.com.

2. Enter SPY (or any ETF that simulates the market).

3. If SMA-200% is positive, it indicates that the market plunge has not been detected and you can skip the following steps.

4. The market is plunging if SMA-50% is more negative than SMA-200%. To illustrate this condition, SMA-200% is -2% and SMA-50% is -5%.

5. Sell most stocks starting with the riskiest ones first such as the ones with negative earnings, high P/Es and/or high Debt/Equity. Obtain this info from Finviz.com by entering the symbol of the stock you own.

6. Conservative investors should sell only those over-priced stocks. Aggressive investors should sell all stocks. Extremely aggressive investors should sell all stocks, buy contra ETFs, and even short stocks. I do not recommend beginners to be aggressive.

When to return to the market (a.k.a. Golden Cross)

Use the above in a reversed sense to detect whether the market has been recovering. However, when the SMA-200% turns positive, I would start buying value stocks (low P/E but the 'E' has to be positive, and/or low Debt/Equity).

1. Bring up Finviz.com.

2. Enter SPY (or any ETF that simulates the market).

3. If SMA-200% is negative, the market is not recovering, and you can skip the following steps.

4. Sell all contra ETFs and close all shorts if you have any.

5. Market recovery is confirmed when SMA-50% is more positive than SMA-200%. To illustrate this condition, SMA-200% is 2% and SMA-50% is 5%. Commit a large percent of cash (or all cash for aggressive investors) to stocks. If you do not know what to buy, buy SPY or an ETF that simulates the market.

Do the above once a month. When the SPY price is closer to SMA actions percentage, perform the above once a week. The charts and data for market timing described in this book are based on SMA-350 (Simple Moving Average) that is more preferable than this simple procedure, but it requires some simple charting.

Appendix 1 – All my books

- Complete the Art of Investing (highly recommended combining most of my books on investing). The Kindle version has over 850 pages (6*9).

- Sector Rotation: 21 Strategies (highly recommended for short-term investors) has more specific chapters on the topic and shares many articles with "Complete the art of investing". Selling Short.

- Best stocks for August, 2020. Best stocks from the recovery of the pandemic. Not a promise: "Best stocks for 2021" available on Dec. 15, 2020 with end-of-year recommendations and another version on June 15, 2021 with mid-year recommendations.

- China: Trade War & Pandemic (highly recommended). Rising China, Falling U.S.A combines the best of many articles from my books on politics. Fall of an Empire: U.S.A. A Nation of No Losers. Can China Say No. Global Economies. Trade War with China. Pandemic.

- Books for today's market: Profit from Coming Market Crash.

- The following books are in a series: Finding Profitable Stocks, Market Timing and Scoring Stocks. Alternate book Using Fidelity.com.

- Books on strategies: "Profit from bull, bear and sideways markets" (Rotation + Momentum + ETF Rotation + trend following), Trading System (similar to printed version of Complete), Swing (Rotation + Momentum), ETF Rotation for Couch Potatoes, Momentum, SuperStocks, Dividend, Penny & Micro Stock, and Retiree.

- Books for advance beginners: Introduce (highly recommended), Billionaire (perfect gift for recent college graduates and they will thank you when they become millionaires), Investing for Beginners, Beat Fund Managers, Profit via ETFs, Buffett, Ideas, Conservative and Top-Down.

- Miscellaneous: Lessons in Investing. Investing Strategies. Buy Low and Sell High. Buy High and sell Higher. Buffettology. Technical Analysis. Trading Stocks.

- Concise Editions and Introduction Editions are available at very low prices and are competitive with books of similar sizes (50 pages) and prices ($3 range).

Most books have paperbacks. Links and offers are subject to change without notice.

Appendix 2 – Complete the Art of Investing

Instead of buying 16 books, why not buy one book (Complete the Art of Investing) consisting of 16 books? Besides saving money and your digital shelve space, it gives you quick reference and concentration on the topic you're currently interested in. It covers most investing topics in investing excluding speculative investing such as currency trading and day trading.
The Kindle version has about 850 pages (6*9), about the size of three books of average size. With the cost of $10 and at least 850 investing ideas, it is about one cent per idea. Most other books have only a few ideas in the entire book

The 16 books

This book "Complete Art of Investing" is divided into 16 books as follows. Click for the link to the book described in Amazon.com. I squeezed more than 3,000 pages into 850 pages by eliminating duplicated information such as evaluating stocks.

Book No.	Amazon.com
1	Beginner & Billionaire
2	Finding Stocks
3	Evaluating Stocks
4	Scoring Stocks
5	Trading Stocks
6	Market Timing
7	Strategies
8	Sector Rotation
9	Insider Trading
10	Penny Stocks & Micro Cap
11	Momentum Investing
12	Dividend Investing
13	Technical Analysis
14	Investing Ideas
15	The Economy
16	Buffettology

The book links are subject to change without notice.

"How to be a billionaire" is for beginners and couch potatoes, who can use the advanced features of this book in the simplest and less time-consuming techniques. Most advance users can skip this section unless they want to use some of the short cuts described.

We start with the basic books Finding Stocks, Evaluate Stocks, Trading Stocks and Market Timing. You can select and start with one of the many styles and strategies in investing such as swing trading and top-down strategy. Many tools are described in other books such as ETFs, technical analysis, covered calls and trading plan.

Many books start with "Why" to lure you to read more and are followed by "How" and then the theory behind the book.
If the book you're reading is beneficial to you, imagine how it would with 850 pages.

#

Most readers' comments are on "Debunk the Myths in Investing", which this book is originally based on. As of 2018, I did not know any of the commentators on my books.

"I skipped ahead to his chapter book 14 (of "Complete the Art of Investing"), Investment Advice just to get a feel of his writing style. His research is phenomenal and doesn't overwhelm with big words or catchy "sales-like" tactics.

I truly believe this ordinary man, Mr. Tony Pow, has a gift of explaining his experience as an investor without the bull crap of trying to make you buy his stuff. He seemingly just wants to share his knowledge, tips, and clarity of definitions for the kind of folks like me who want to understand something FIRST before jumping in with emotions of trying to make a boat load of money. I like the technical analysis side he brings.

Mr. Tony Pow talks about hidden gems in his book; well....quite frankly, he is a hidden gem. Thank you and I will also post my comments about this author to my Facebook page!" – JB on this book.

"Excellent book, recommend to all investors... great knowledge. It has fine-tuned my investing strategies... Your book is hard to set aside, as I read it all the time learning good techniques and analysis of stocks, ETF... Since I purchased your book in March, I have underlined, highlighted and placed tabs on top of pages for quick reference." – Aileron on this book.

"Tony, I just finished reading your 2nd edition. It's my pleasure to report that I found it most interesting. You're welcome to use this blurb if you like:

Debunk the Myths in Investing is an all-encompassing look at not only the most salient factors influencing markets and investors, but also a from-the-trenches look at many of the misconceptions and mistakes too many investors make. Reading this book may save not only time and aggravation but money as well!"

Joseph Shaefer, CEO, Stanford Wealth Management LLC.

"Tony, Great work!" from James and Chris, who are portfolio managers.

"'Debunk the Myths in Investing' is a comprehensive book on investing that deals with many aspects of this tense profession in which with a lot of knowledge and a bit of luck (or vice versa) one can greatly benefit...

Therefore 'Debunk the Myths in Investing' is an interesting book that on its 500 pages offer a lot of knowledge related to investing world and many practical advice, so I can recommend its reading if you're interested in this topic."
- Denis Vukosav, Top 500 Reviewers at Amazon.com.

"490 pages (Debunk) of a genius's ranting and hypothesis with various theories throughout, written light-heartedly with ample doses of humor...Yes, the myth of not being able to profitably time the market is BUSTED...

One might ask... Why is he giving away the results of his hard-earned research for only $20? He states that his children are not interested in investing and wants to share his efforts with the world." - Abe Agoda.

"Excellent book, recommend to all investors... great knowledge. It has fine-tuned my investing strategies... Your book is hard to set aside, as I read it all the time learning good techniques and analysis of stocks, ETF... Since I purchased your book in March, I have underlined, highlighted and placed tabs on top of pages for quick reference." - Aileron on this book.

"Great stuff, Tony. It's great to meet experienced traders such as yourself. I had a browse through the book and think your method is a little more refined than mine."
"Your strategy is very rules based and solid. I sometimes envy people who have developed something like this."

Making 50% in one month

I claim to have the best one-month performance ever for recommending 8 or more stocks without using options and leverage. My following return is 57% in a month or 621% annualized. They are slightly different as I calculated the average from the averages of three different accounts. The average buy date is 12/26/18 and the "current date" is 01/28/19.

The performance may not be repeated. I will use the same screen for the coming years and even the expected 10% (or 120% annualized) is very good.

I used the same screen for searching stock candidates. I spent a total of about 20 hours from Dec. 15, 2018 to Jan. 5, 2019.

Stock	Buy Price	Sold or Current Price	Buy date	Sold or Current date	Profit %	Profit % Ann.	Status
CHK	2.13	2.99	01/03/09	01/18/19	40%	982%	Sold
MNK	16.41	21.45	01/03/19	01/25/19	31%	510%	Sold
MNK	16.43	21.45	01/03/19	01/25/19	31%	507%	Sold
NNBR	5.68	8.58	12/26/18	01/28/19	51%	565%	
NNBR	5.72	8.58	12/26/18	01/28/19	66%	727%	
ESTE	4.35	6.45	12/26/18	01/18/19	48%	766%	Sold
LCI	4.61	8.29	12/21/18	01/28/19	80%	767%	
MDR	8.01	9.13	01/08/19	01/28/19	14%	255%	
YRCW	3.29	5.78	12/21/18	01/28/19	76%	727%	
YRCW	3.26	5.78	12/21/18	01/28/19	77%	742%	
ASRT	3.56	4.18	12/26/18	01/28/19	17%	193%	
UTCC	7.13	11.00	12/26/18	01/28/19	54%	600%	
YRCW	2.92	5.78	12/26/18	01/28/19	98%	1083%	

Best one-year return

I claim to have the best-performed article in Seeking Alpha history, an investing site, for recommending 15 or more stocks in one year after the publish date without using options and leverage.

https://seekingalpha.com/article/1095671-amazing-returns-velti-alcatel-lucent-alpha-natural-resources

Sector Rotation: 21 Strategies

- On 5/26/2020, I searched for "Sector Rotation" under Amazon's Book. They are listed in the same order except my book Sector Rotation: 21 Strategies. All data particular to Price and Size are subjected to changes without notice.

Book	Date	Size[1]	Kindle $[1]	Hard $
Sector Rotation: 21 Strategies	**05/2020**	**425**	**$9.95**	$24.95
Super Sectors	09/2010	289	$26.39	$49.95

Dual Momentum Investing	11/2014	240	$40.40	$42.20
Sector Investing	05/1996	260		$29.94
Sector Trading Strategies	08/2007	164	$26.39	$16.66
The Sector Strategist	03/2012	225	$26.39	$44.96
ETF Rotation	10/2012	125	**$9.95**	**$14.99**
Optimal... Sector Rotation	07/2015	80		$44.07

[1] From Amazon on size and prices as of 5/25/2020.

My book won in all categories except the price for hard copy in one. However, my book won as the lowest cost per page by a wide margin. In addition, as of 5/2020 I bet that no author besides me made over 4 times using sector rotation starting the amount more than his yearly salary then.

- I have **21** strategies in sector rotation while most books have only one. It ranges from simple rotation of a stock ETF and cash for beginners to many advanced strategies for experts. Most other books have one or two strategies.
- Andrew, a contributor on Sector Rotation article at Seeking Alpha, said, "Great stuff, Tony. It's great to meet experienced traders such as yourself. I had a browse through the book and think your method is a little more refined than mine."
- "You have written the book in a way that makes good and logical sense." Bill.
- Do not be fooled by past performances. Just check the recent performance of the top 50 stocks selected by IBD in the last five years. The mediocre result (hopefully it will change) could be due to too many followers and/or there is no evergreen strategy. I seldom heard the fantastic results from the followers of O'Neil, our greatest chartist. The adaptive strategy of this book shows you how to select the most profitable strategy for the current market.
- I switched most (if not all) my sector funds in April, 2000 from technology sectors to traditional sectors (better to money market fund). We can reduce losses by spotting market plunges and the sector trend.

My motivation to write this book is sharing my experiences, both bad and good. I provide simple-to-follow techniques using the free (or low-cost) resources available to us. I have been successful in investing for decades. I am enjoying a comfortable financial life. I do not hold back my 'secrets' as my children are not interested in investing. If you are looking how to make 100% return overnight, there are many other books claiming to do so and this book is not for you. This book describes how to be a 'turtle' investor making fortune gradually and surely. Be warned that many books written by authors who have never make money in the stock market.

Best stocks to buy as of July, 2021

We care about performance only. Not considering dividends and fees, my last three books in this series have beaten the SPY (the market to most) by **110%, 71% and 25%** from the publish date to 07/01/2021.

My new book in this series titled "Best stocks to buy as of July, 2021" has been just released in Amazon.com on 07/15/2021. For more description, please click here, or type the following in your browser: https://www.amazon.com/dp/B099KQ9DSV

Book	Stocks	Return	Ann.	Beat SPY by
Best Book for 2021 2nd Edition	10	20%	52%	110%
Best Book for 2021	4	29%	52%	71%
Best Book to Buy from Aug, 2020	14	42%	45%	25%
Avg.	9	31%	50%	69%

The following are not promises. I plan to release a new book in this series titled "Best Stocks" on 12/15 each year. I may release my techniques for retail investors and institution investors for one-time charges. Contact me at pow_tony@yahoo.com if you are interested.

Appendix 3 - ETFs / Mutual Funds

What is an ETF

ETFs have basic differences from mutual funds: 1. Lower management expenses, 2. Trade ETFs same as stocks, and 3. Usually more diversified but not more selective than the related mutual funds such as NOBL vs FRDPX.

The major classifications of ETFs are 1. Simulating an index such as SPY, QQQ and DIA, 2. Simulating a sector such as XLE and SOXX, 3. Simulating an asset class such as GLD and SLV, 4. Simulating a country or a group of countries such as EWC and FXI, 5. Managed by a manager(s) such as ARKK, 6. Betting a market or sector to go down such as SH and PSQ, and 7. Leveraged (not recommended for beginners).

Fidelity: Index ETFs (https://www.fidelity.com/etfs/overview).
Wikipedia on ETF (http://en.wikipedia.org/wiki/Exchange-traded_fund).

List of ETFs
ETF database (Recommended): http://etfdb.com/
ETF Bloomberg: http://www.bloomberg.com/markets/etfs/
ETF Trends: http://www.etftrends.com/
A list of ETFs. Seeking Alpha.
http://etf.stock-encyclopedia.com/category/)
A list of contra ETFs (or bear ETFs)
http://www.tradermike.net/inverse-short-etfs-bearish-etf-funds/
Misc.: ETFGuide, ETFReplay

Fidelity low-cost index funds:
https://www.youtube.com/watch?v=zpKi4_IJvlY
Fidelity Annuity funds with performance data.
http://fundresearch.fidelity.com/annuities/category-performance-annual-total-returns-quarterly/FPRAI?refann=005

Other resources
Most subscription services offer research on ETFs. IBD has a strategy dedicated to ETFs and so does AAII to name a couple. Seeking Alpha has extensive resources for ETF including an ETF screener and investing ideas. So is ETFdb.

Not all ETFs are created equal
Check their performances and their expenses.

When to use or not to use ETFs

I prefer sector mutual funds in some industries, as they have many bad stocks such as drug industry, banks, miners and insurers. Most mutual funds cannot time the market.

When you believe a sector is heading up (or contra ETF for heading down), but you do not have time to do research on specific stocks, buy an ETF for the sector; it is same for the market.

Half ETF

Taking out half of the stocks that score below the average in an index ETF could beat the same full ETF itself. I call it HETF (half the ETF). You heard it here first.

To illustrate, sort the expected P/E (not including stocks with negative earnings) in ascending order and only include the stocks on the first half. Add more fundamental metrics. It will take a few minutes.

Disadvantages of ETFs

- When you have two stocks in a sector ETF one good one and one bad one, the ETF treats them the same. Stock pickers would buy the one that has a better appreciation potential.
- Sometimes the return could be misleading due to stock rotation. To illustrate this, on August 29, 2012, SHLD was replaced by LYB in a sector fund. SHLD was down by 4% and LYB was up by 4% primarily due to the switch. Unless you sell and buy at the right time (which is impossible), your return would not match the ETF's returns due to the replacement.
- Ensure the performance matches the corresponding index; it is hard due to excluding dividends.

Advantages of ETFs
- We have demonstrated that you can beat the market by using market timing. Between 2000 and Nov., 2013, you only exit and reenter the market 3 times and the result is astonishing.
- It is easy to rotate a sector vs. buying/selling all of the stocks in this sector. Rotating a sector is the same as trading a stock.
- The risk is spread out, and your portfolio is diversified especially for a market ETF or buying three or more ETFs in different sectors.
- Periodically the bad stocks in most funds are replaced by better stocks.
- Eliminate the time in researching stocks.

Leveraged ETFs
I do not recommend them. Some are 2x, 3x and even higher. They're too risky for beginners. However, when you are very sure or your tested strategy has very low drawdown, you may want to use them to improve performance. Most leveraged ETFs and contra ETFs have higher fees.

My basic ETF tables
I include some contra ETFs, mutual funds and Fidelity's annuity. Some of these may be interesting to you. Most Vanguard's ETFs have lower fees.

ETFs and funds come and go. Some ideas and classifications are my own interpretation. Refer to ETFdb for updated information. Not responsible for any error. Check out the ETF or fund before you take any action.

I prefer VFINX over SPY for the lower fees; both simulate the S&P 500 index. The stocks in the ETF can be either equally weighed or weighed by market caps. The latter is more like using momentum strategy, as the rising stocks usually have larger market caps. The index usually kicks out some poor-performing stocks and replaced them with better stocks. These ETFs are suited for long-term investing without constant reviews.

Table by market cap:

Category	ETF	Mutual Funds	Fidelity's Annuity	Contra ETF	Alternate
Size:					
Large Cap	DIA			DOG	
	SPY			SH	VFINX FXAIX VOO
	QQQ			PSQ	FNCMX
	RYH				
Blend	IWD	BEQGX			
Growth	SPYG	FBGRX			FSPGX
Value	SPYV	DOGGX			FLCOX
Dividend	NOBL	FRDPX			
	VYM				
Mid Cap			FNBSC	MYY	
Blend	MDY	VSEQX			
Growth		STDIX			
		BPTRX			
Value		FSMVX			
Small Cap			FPRGC	SBB	FSSNX

Blend	IWM	HDPSX			
Growth		PRDSX			FECGX
Value		SKSEX			FISVX
Micro	IWC				
Multi					
Blend		VDEOX			
Growth		VHCOX			
Value		TCLCX			
Total					FSKAX VTI
Bond					
Long Term (20)	VLV	BTTTX		TBF	
Mid Term (7 – 10)	VCIT	FSTGX			
Short Term (1 – 3 yrs.)	VCSH	THOPX			
Total	BOND	PONDX			
Corp Invest Grade	VCIT	NTHEX			
High Yield (junk)	PHB	SPHIX			
Muni	MUB	Check state			
Special situation					
Buy back	PKW				

Table by sectors:

Sector	ETF	Mutual Funds	Fidelity's Annuity
Banking[1]		FSRBK	
Regional	IAT		
Biotech	IBB	FBIOX	
	XBI	Large	
Consumer Dis.	XLY	FSCPX	FVHAC
Consumer Staple	XLP	FDFAX	FCSAC
Finance	KIE	FIDSX	FONNC
	IYF		
Energy	XLE	FSENX	FJLLC

Energy Service		FSESX	
Gold	GLD	FSAGX	BAR
Gold Miner	GDX	VGPMX	
Health Care	IYH	FSPHX	FPDRC
	VHT	VGHCX	
House Builder	ITB	FSHOX	
	ITB	Perform	
Industrial	IYJ	FCYIX	FBALC
Material	VAW	FSDPX	GSG
	IYM		
Oil	USO		
Oil Service	OIH	FSESX	
Oil Exploration	XOP		
Real Estate	VNQ	FRIFX	FFWLC
REIT	VNQ		
Retail	RTH	FSRPX	
	XRT		
Regional bank	KRE	FSRBX	
Semi Conduct	SMH		
Software	XSW	FSCSX	
	IGV		
Technology	XLK	FSPTX	FYENC
	FDN	FBSOX	
		ROGSX	
Telecomm.	VOX	FSTCX	FVTAC
Transport	XTN		
	IYT		
Utilities	XLU	FSUTX	FKMSC
Wireless		FWRLX	

Footnote. [1] Also check Finance.

Table by countries outside the USA:

Country	ETF	Mutual Funds	Fidelity's Annuity	Alternate
Australia	EWA			
Brazil	EWZ			
Canada	EWC	FICDX		
China	FXI	FHKCX		
EAFE	EFA			

Emerging	VWO	FEMEX	FEMAC	FPADX
Europe	VGK	FIEUX		
Global	KXI	PGVFX		
Greece	GREK			
India	INDY	MINDX		
Indonesia	EIDO			
Latin America	ILF	FLATX		
Nordic		FNORX		
Hong Kong	EWH			
Japan	EWJ	FJPNX		
S. Africa	EZA			
S. Korea	EWY	MAKOX		
Singapore	EWS			
Taiwan	EWT			
	TUR			
United Kingdom	EWU			
Foreign:				
Combination				
Intern. Div.	IDV			FTIHX
Small Cap	SCZ			
Value	EFV			
Europe	VGK			

Quick analysis of ETFs

Evaluate an ETF

ETFs are a basket of stocks according to the market, a specific sector, country or a specific theme.

Yahoo!Finance used to give the P/E of an ETF. Try to get it from ETFdb.com. Enter the symbol of the ETF such as XLU, and then select Valuation. If it is below 15 and above zero, it could be a value ETF. Also, if the current price is lower than its NAV, it is sold at a discount (or premium vice versa). Compare its YTD Return to SPY's.

Alternatively, get similar info from http://www.multpl.com/. In addition, this web site provides the following metrics: Shiller P/E, Price/Sales, and Price/Book.

From Finviz.com, enter the ETF symbol. If SMA-20%, SMA-50% and SMA-200% are all positive, most likely the ETF is in an uptrend. To illustrate, SMA-200 is Simple Moving Average for the last 200 trading sessions (no trading on weekends and specific holidays). The percent is how much the stock price of the ETF is above the SMA. If the percent is negative, it means the stock price is below the SMA.

If your average holding period of your stocks is about 50 days, SMA-50% is more appropriate to you.

If RSI(14) > 65, it is probably over-sold; if it is < 30, it is probably under-sold (indicating value).

In addition, ensure the ETF's average volume is high (I suggest more than 10,000 shares), the market cap is more than 300 M, and it has low fees. Most popular ETFs have these characteristics. Beginners should avoid leveraged ETFs.

How to determine if the sector has been recovered

It is easier to profit by following the uptrend of an ETF using the above info. It is hard to detect when the bottom of an ETF has been reached. If SMA-20%, SMA-50% and SMA-200% are all positive, most likely the ETF is in an uptrend or it has recovered. It does not always happen as predicted, so use stops to protect your investment.

An example

First, determine whether the market is risky. Most beginners should not invest in a risky market. Advanced investors can bet against the market or a specific sector by buying contra ETFs or puts.

Next, you want to limit the number of sector ETFs by selecting those that are either in an uptrend or hitting bottom (bottom is hard to predict). Personally I prefer sectors with long-term uptrends (indicated by articles found in many web sites including cnnfn.com and Seeking Alpha.

For illustration purposes only for deteriorating market conditions, I would select the following ETFs: SPY (simulating the market based on large companies) and XLP (consumer staples). XLP should perform better than XLY (consumer discretionary) during a recession as those products are the necessities.

Technical indicators such as SMA-50 (Simple Moving Average for the last 50 sessions), SMA-200 and RSI(14) are obtained from Finviz.com and the rest are obtained from Yahoo!Finance.com. After you buy the ETF, use a stop loss to protect your investment. For example, bio tech sector moved up for many months until it crashed in 2015. Change the stop loss value every month to protect your gains in this case.

As of 2/5/2016	SPY	XLP (staples)	XLY (discret.)
Price	190	50	71
NAV	192	50	73
• Technical			
SMA-50	-4%	0%	-7%
SMA-200	-6%	2%	-7%
RSI(14)	44	50	36
Other	Double bottom at $186		
• Fundamental			
P/E	17	20	19
Yield	2.1%	2.5%	1.5%
YTD return	-5%	0.5%	-5%
Net asset	174 B	9 B	10 B

Explanation

- The figures may not be identical among web sites due to the dates they are using.
- XLY has best discount among the 3 ETFs as most investors believe a recession is coming.
- XLP has less down trend among the 3 ETFs as expected.
- XLY is more undersold among the three as expected.
- Double bottom is a technical pattern that indicates the stock would surge upward.
- SPY has a better value according to its P/E.
- XLY's dividend is the least among the three as they have more tech companies in the ETF. They have to plow back the profits to research and development.
- XLP has the best YTD return among the three.
- As long as the asset is above 500 M (200 M for specialized ETFs), it is fine and all three pass this mark.

There are many metrics such as Debt/Equity not readily available from most web sites. Many sites list the top holdings of a specific ETF. Just average the metrics of the top ten or so of its stock holdings.

Appendix 4 - Our window to the investing world

- **General**
  Wikipedia / Investopedia /Yahoo!Finance / MarketWatch / Cnnfn / Morningstar /CNBC / Bloomberg / WSJ / Barron's / Motley Fool / TheStreet
- **Evaluate stocks**
  Finviz / SeekingAlpha / MSN Money / Zacks / Daily Finance / ADR / Fidelity / Earnings Impact / OpenInsider / NYSE / NASDAQ / SEC / SEC for 10K and 10Q (quarterly) reports required to file for listed stocks in major exchanges.
- **Charts**
  BigCharts / FreeStockCharts / StockCharts /
- **Screens**
  Yahoo!Finance / Finviz / CNBC / Morningstar /
- **Besides stocks**
  123Jump / Hoover's Online / FINRA Bond Market Data / REIT / Commodity Futures / Option Industry
  Nolo (estate planning) / AARP /
- **Vendors**
  AAII / Zacks / IBD / GuruFocus / VectorVest / Fidelity / Interactive Brokers / Merrill Lynch /
- **Economy.**
  Econday / EcoconStats / Federal Reserve / Economist /
- **Misc.**
  Dow Jones Indices / Russell / Wilshire / IRS / Wikinvest / ETF Database / ETF Trends /

#Filler: Honey, my book can play music.

https://www.youtube.com/watch?v=HxGT5z6d-GA&list=PLMZa6mP7jZ2b1otqG4tfbgZpLEdh6YiNF

It may cut down commercials by casting it to TV.

www.ingramcontent.com/pod-product-compliance
Lightning Source LLC
Chambersburg PA
CBHW071816170526
45167CB00003B/1325